Big Book of P

MW01010202

Table of Contents

Managing Editor: Cindy Daoust

Editor at Large: Diane Badden

Copy Editors: Tazmen Carlisle, Amy Kirtley-Hill, Karen L. Mayworth, Kristy Parton, Debbie Shoffner, Cathy Edwards Simrell

Cover Artist: Clevell Harris

Art Coordinator: Theresa Lewis Goode

Artists: Pam Crane, Theresa Lewis Goode, Clevell Harris, Ivy L. Koonce, Sheila Krill, Clint Moore, Greg D. Rieves, Rebecca Saunders, Barry Slate, Donna K. Teal

Contributing Artist: Cathie Carter

4

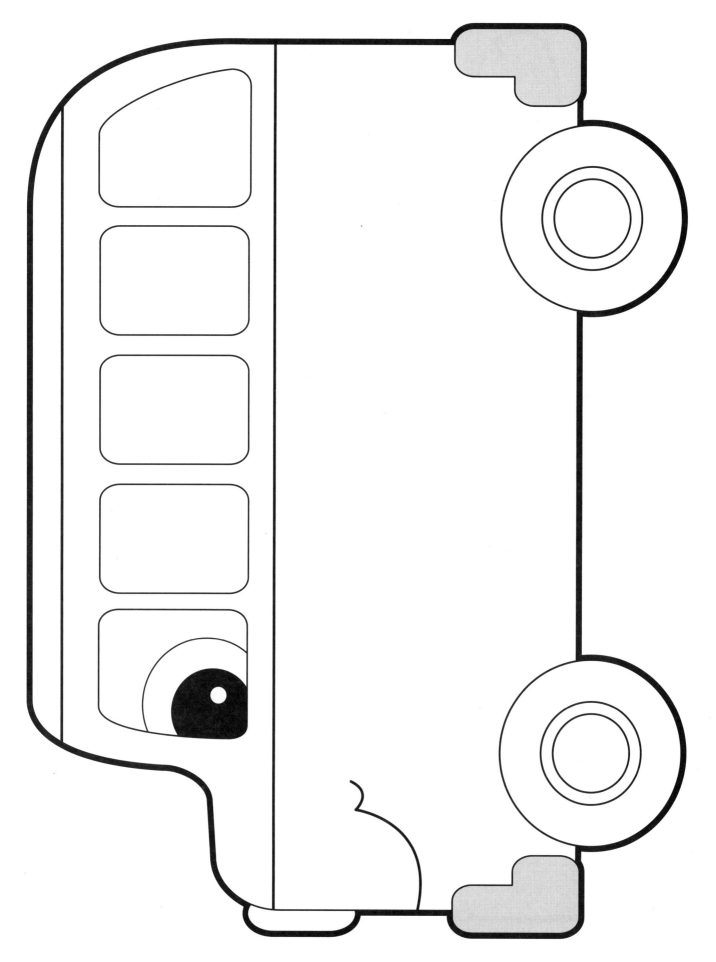

6 ©The Education Center, Inc. • *Big Book of Patterns* • TEC61225

Children

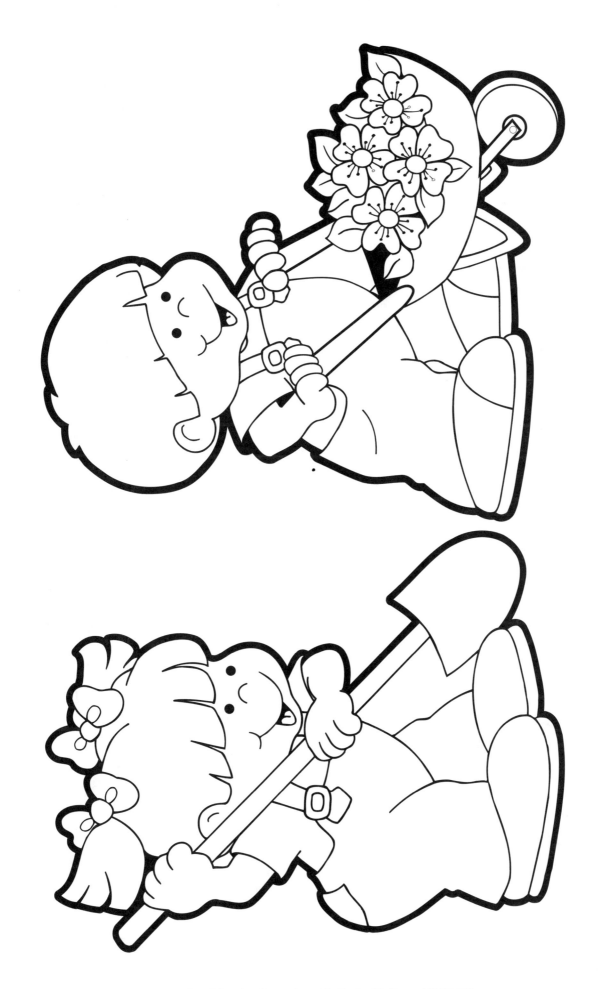

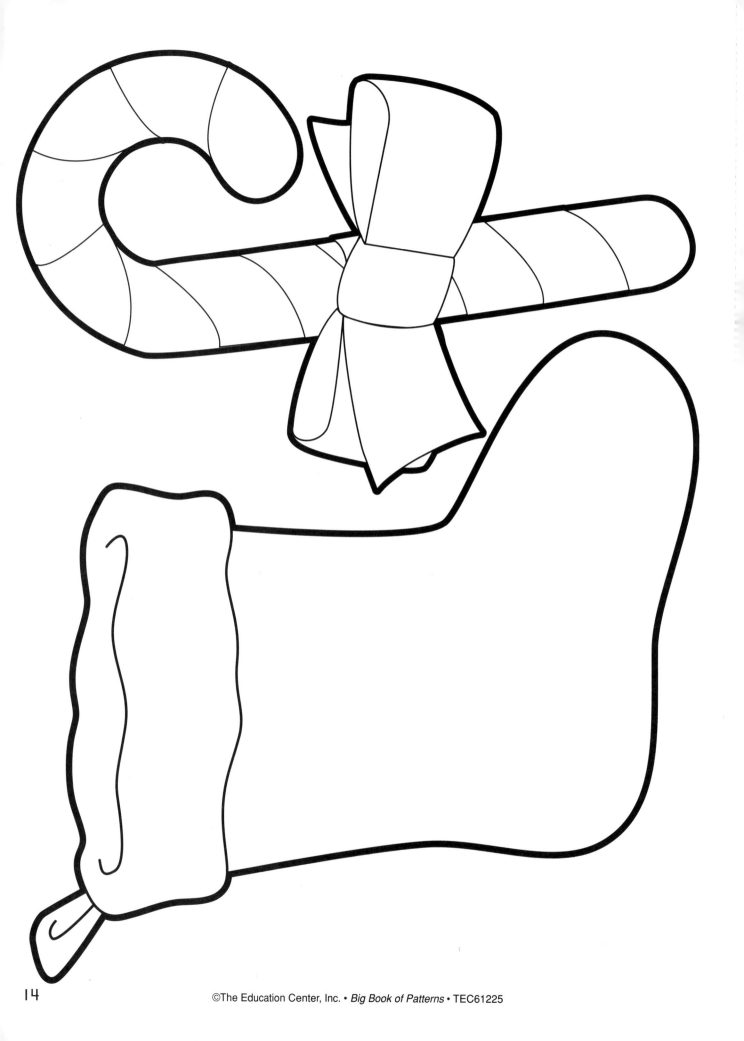

14   ©The Education Center, Inc. • *Big Book of Patterns* • TEC61225

16

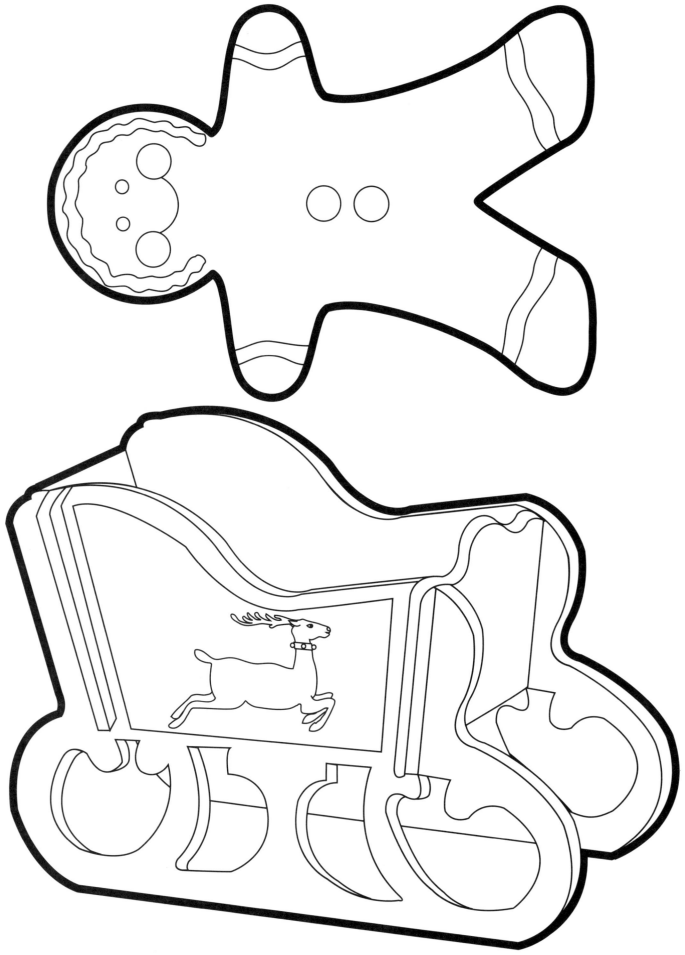

20

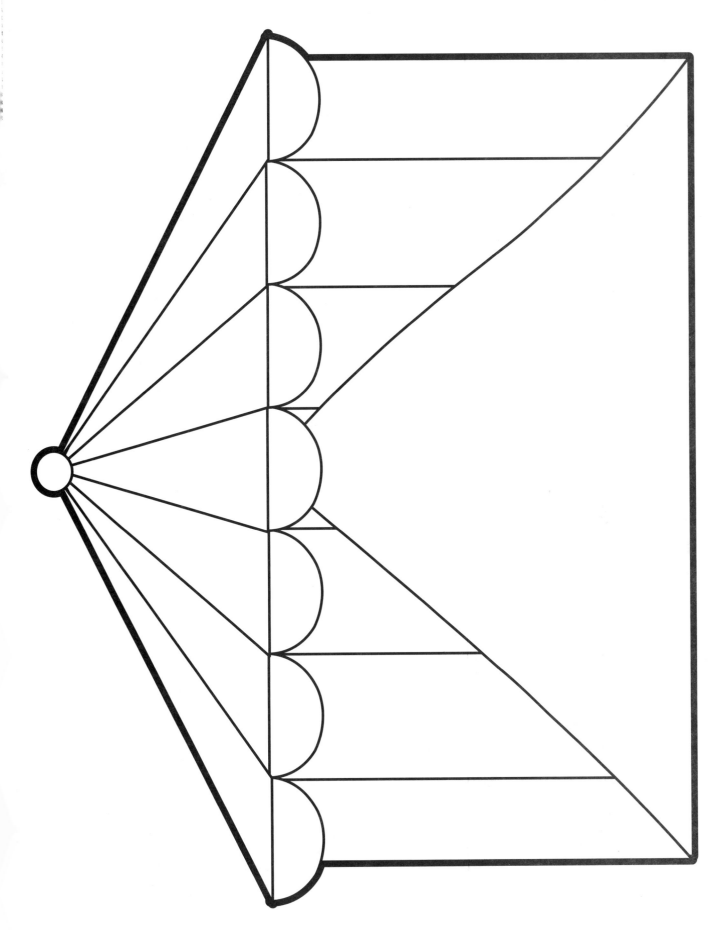

22

24

28   ©The Education Center, Inc. • *Big Book of Patterns* • TEC61225

Clothing

30 ©The Education Center, Inc. • *Big Book of Patterns* • TEC61225

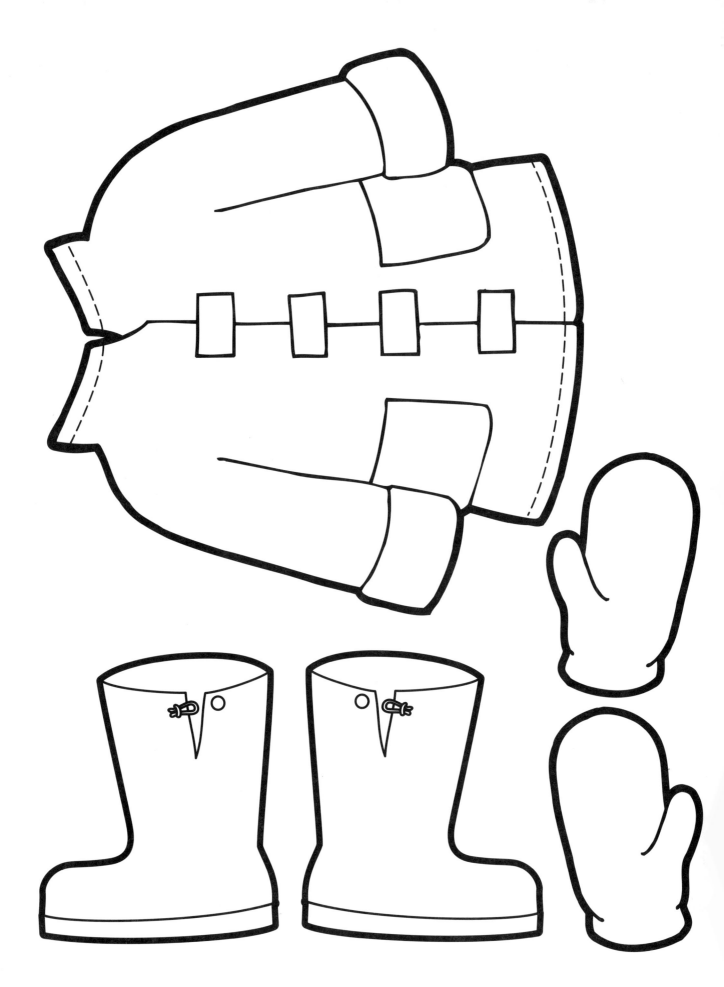

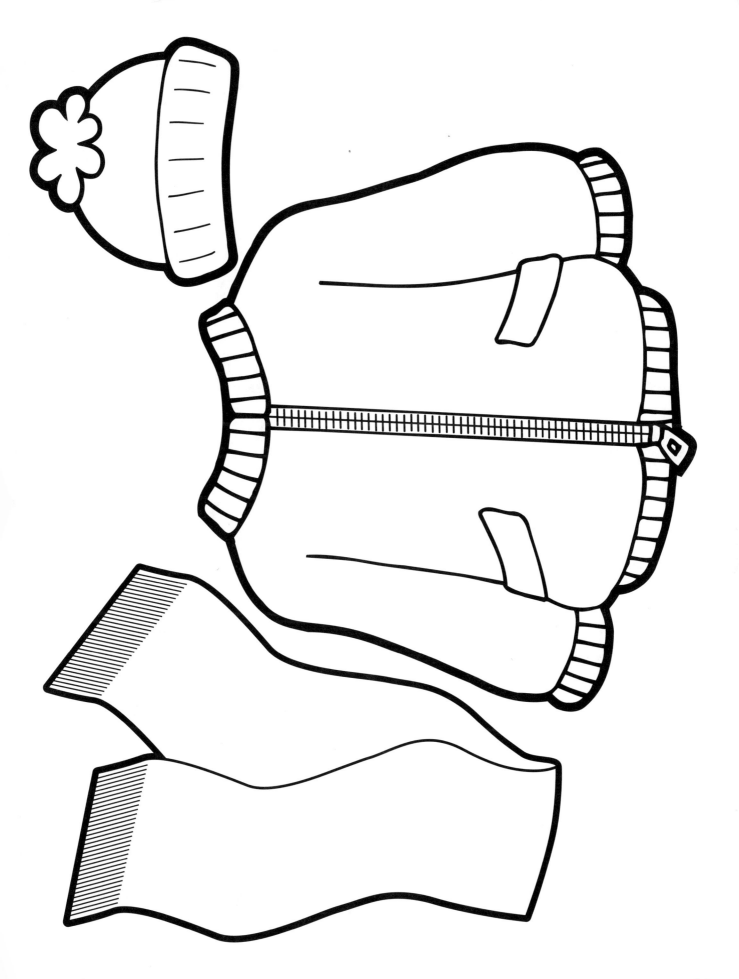

Columbus Day

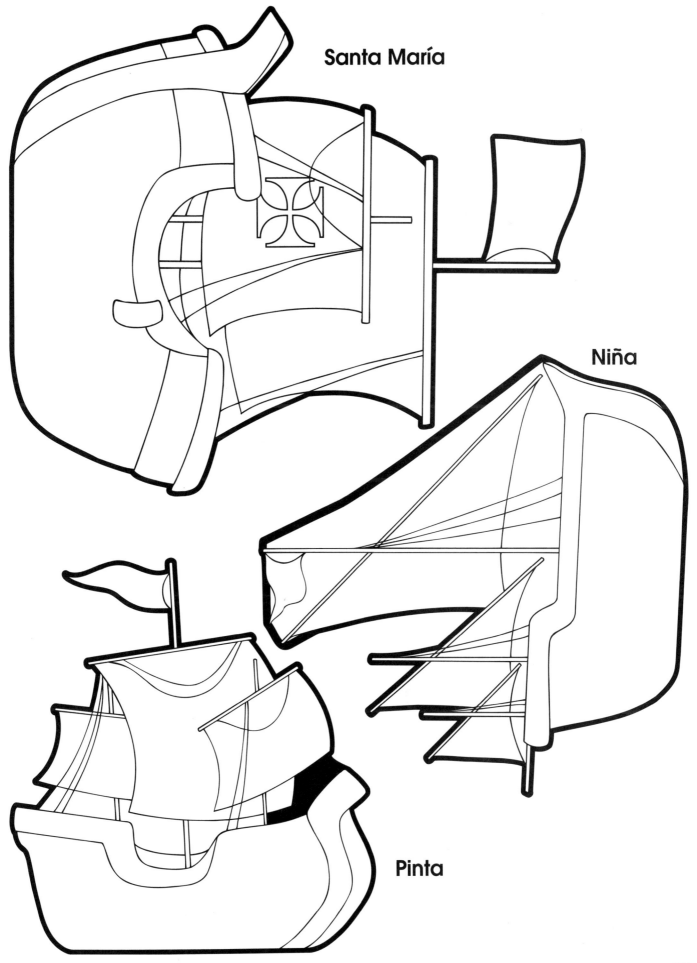

Santa María

Niña

Pinta

Community Helpers

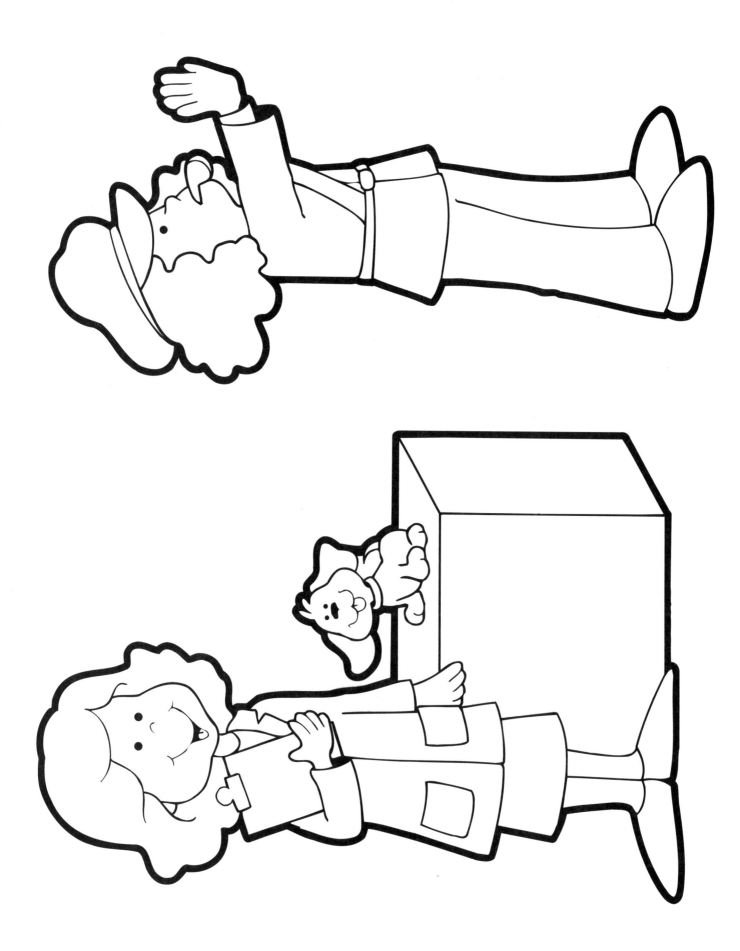

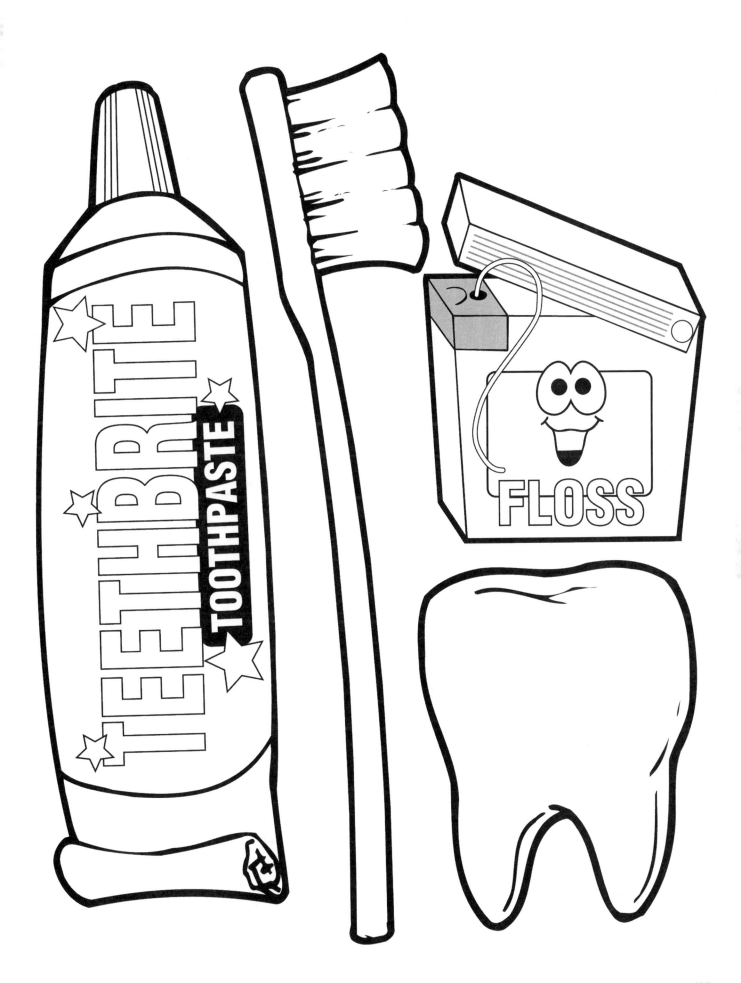

Dinosaurs

46

48

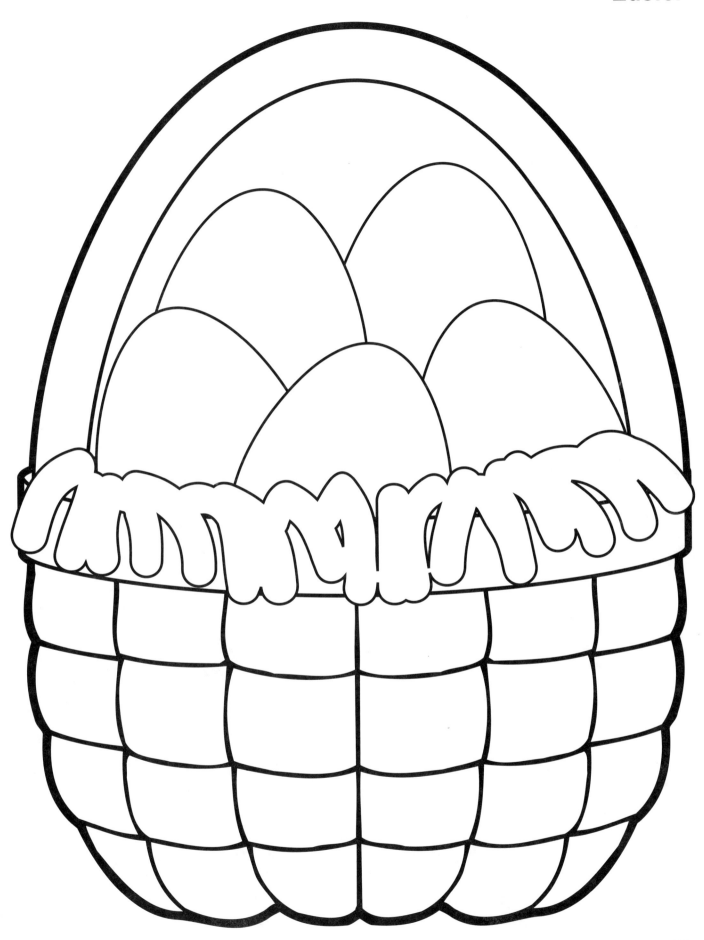

Fall

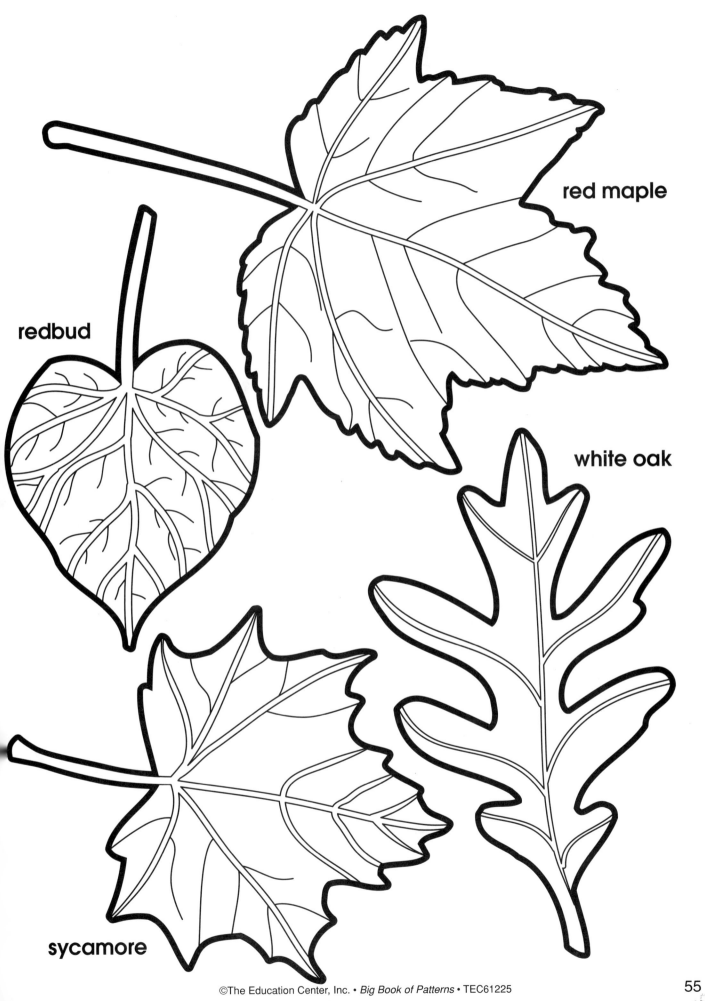

red maple

redbud

white oak

sycamore

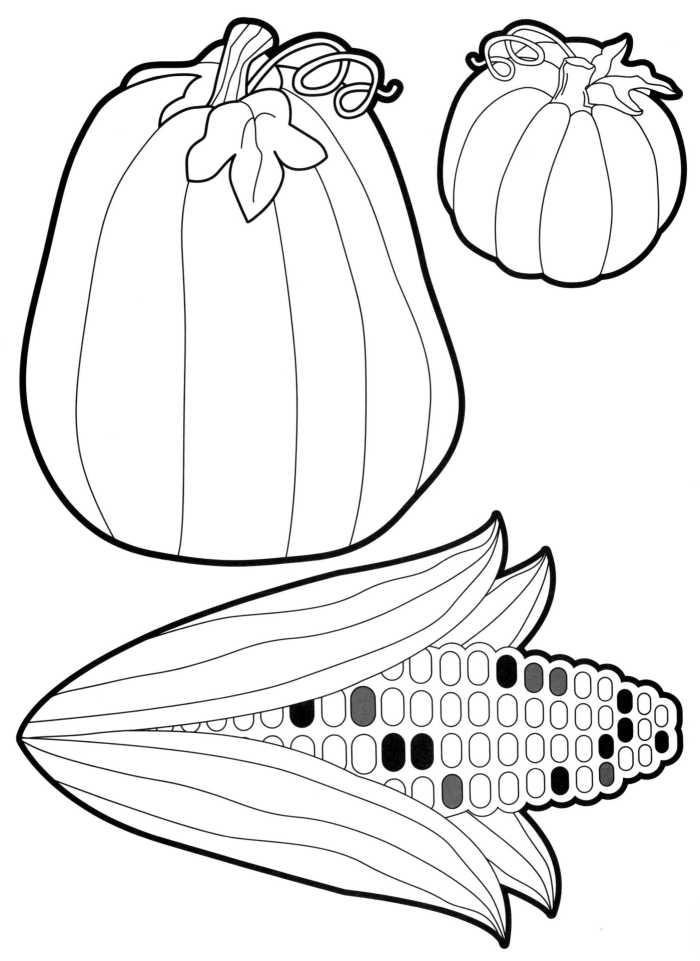

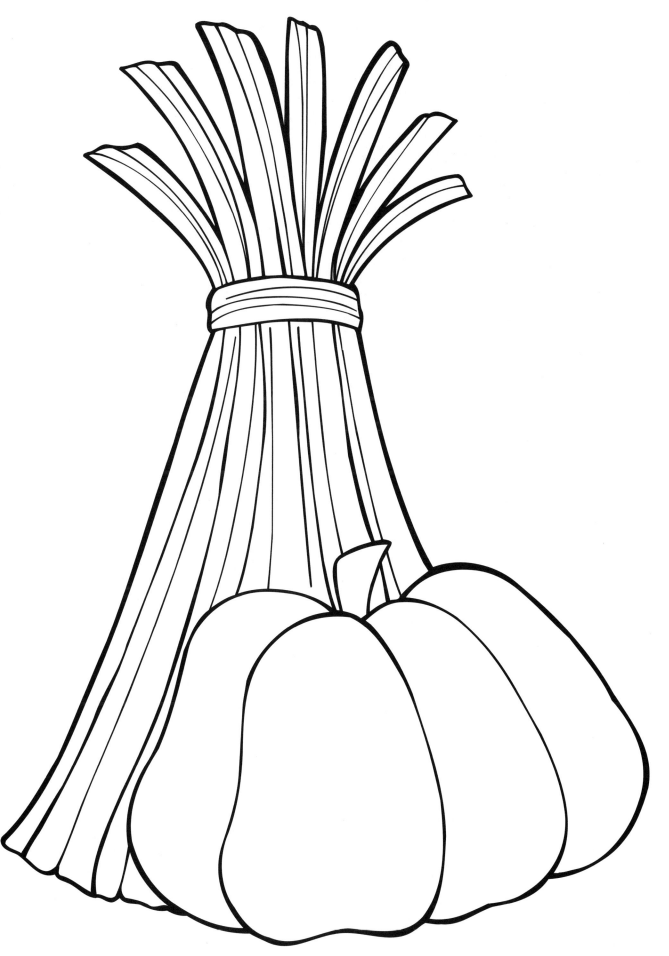

Farm

Food

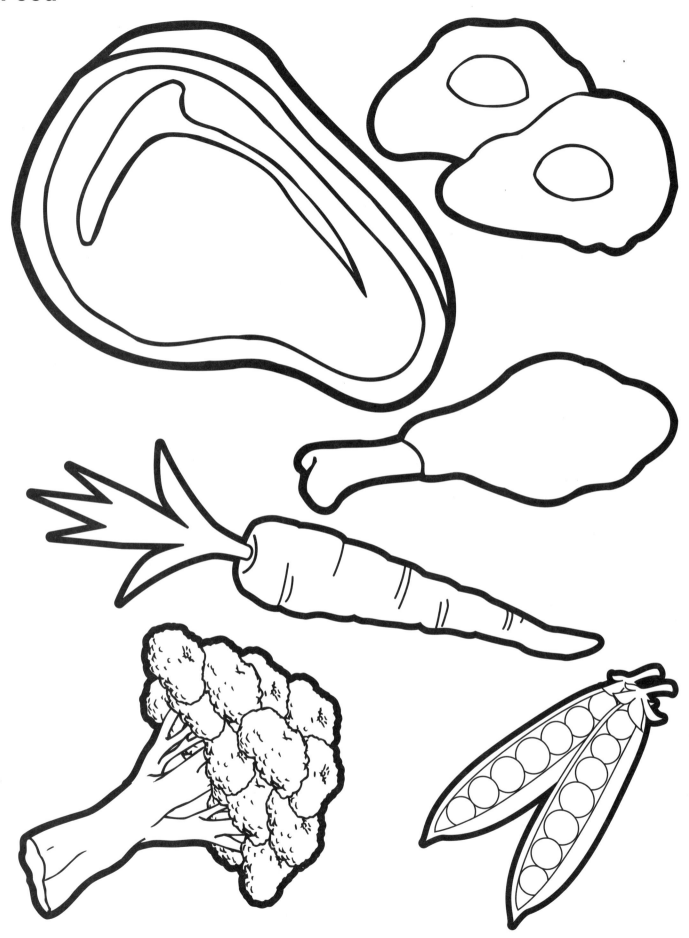

2 CUP

1 1/2 CUP

1 CUP

1/2 CUP

Fourth of July

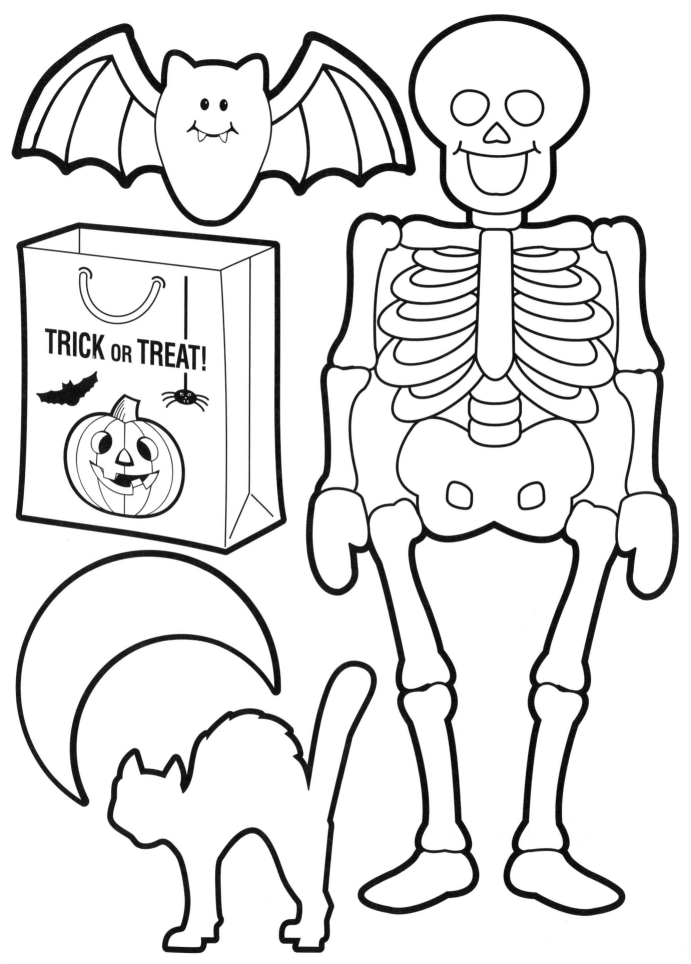

TRICK OR TREAT!

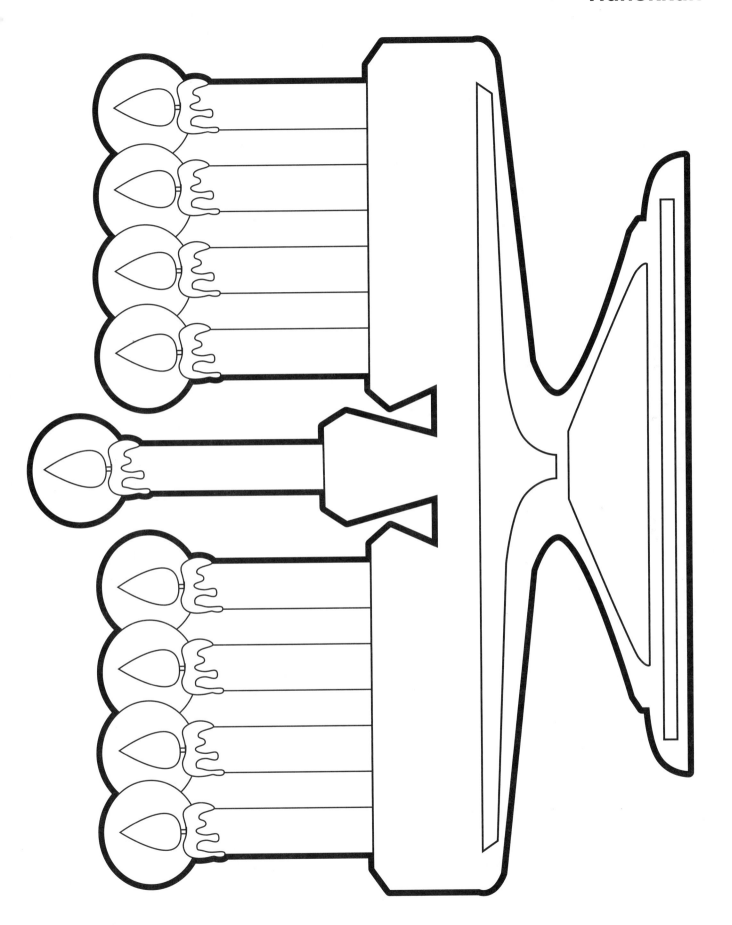

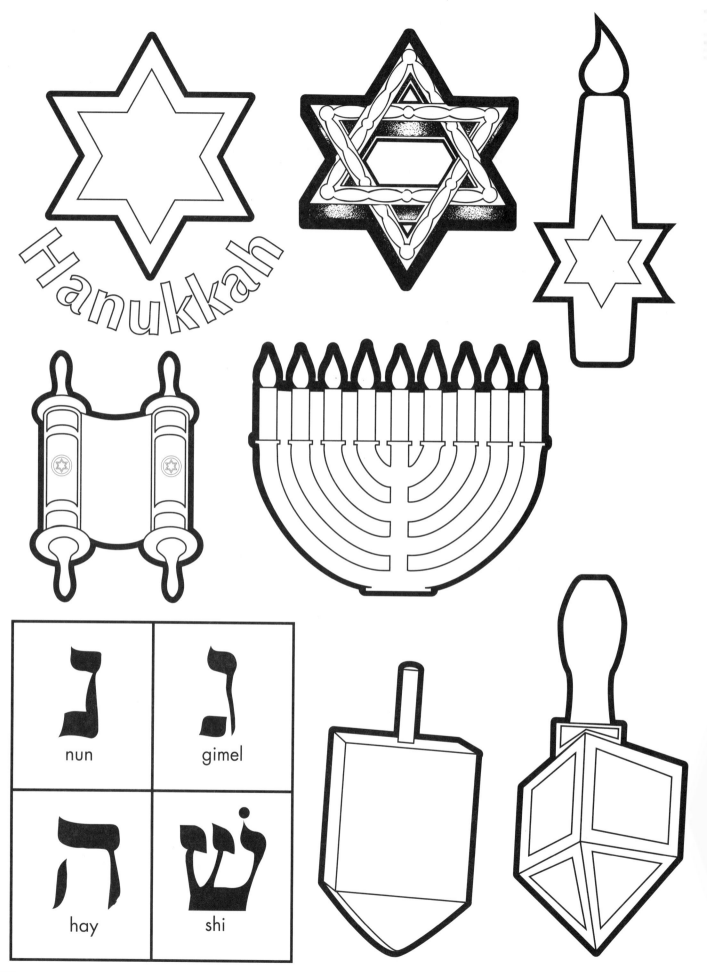

Hanukkah

nun

gimel

hay

shi

©The Education Center, Inc. • *Big Book of Patterns* • TEC61225

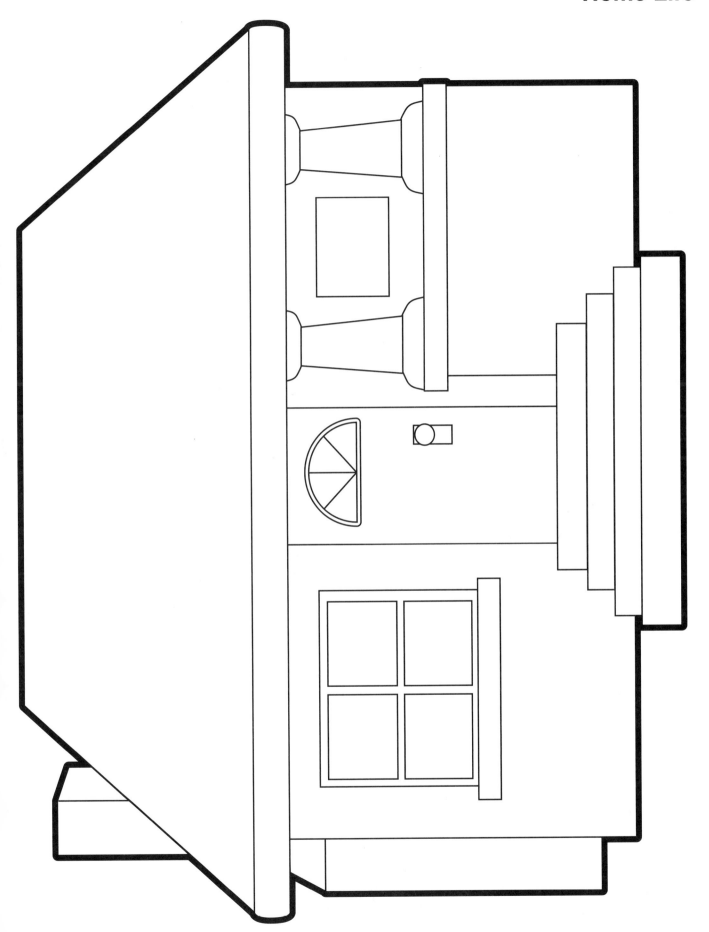

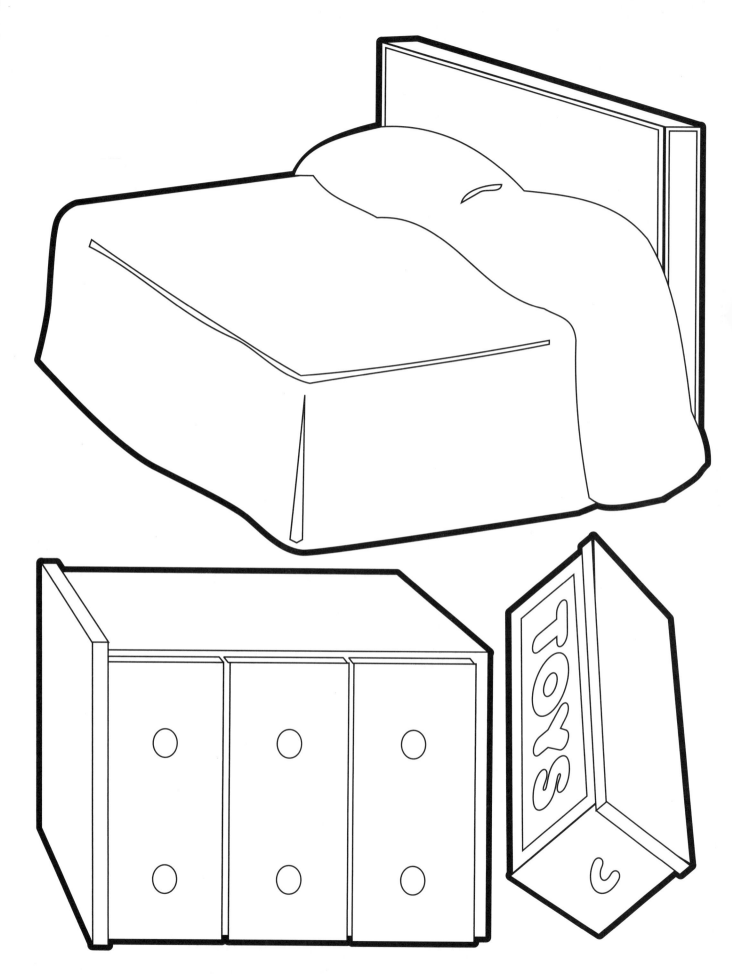

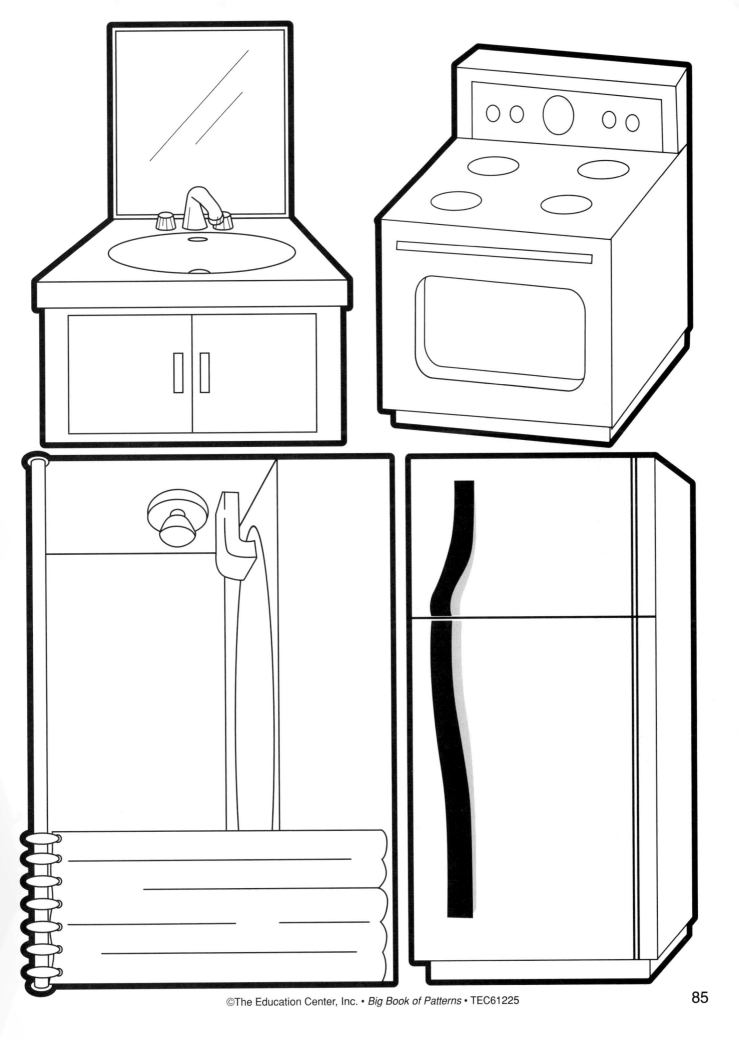

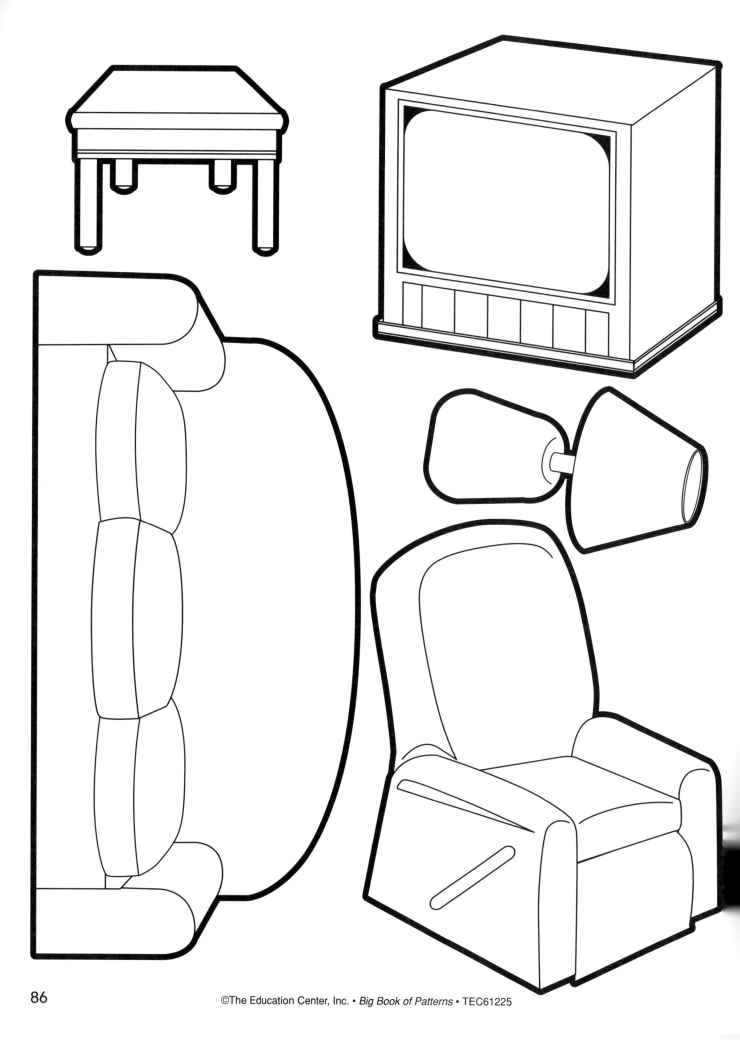

Ice Cream

Insects

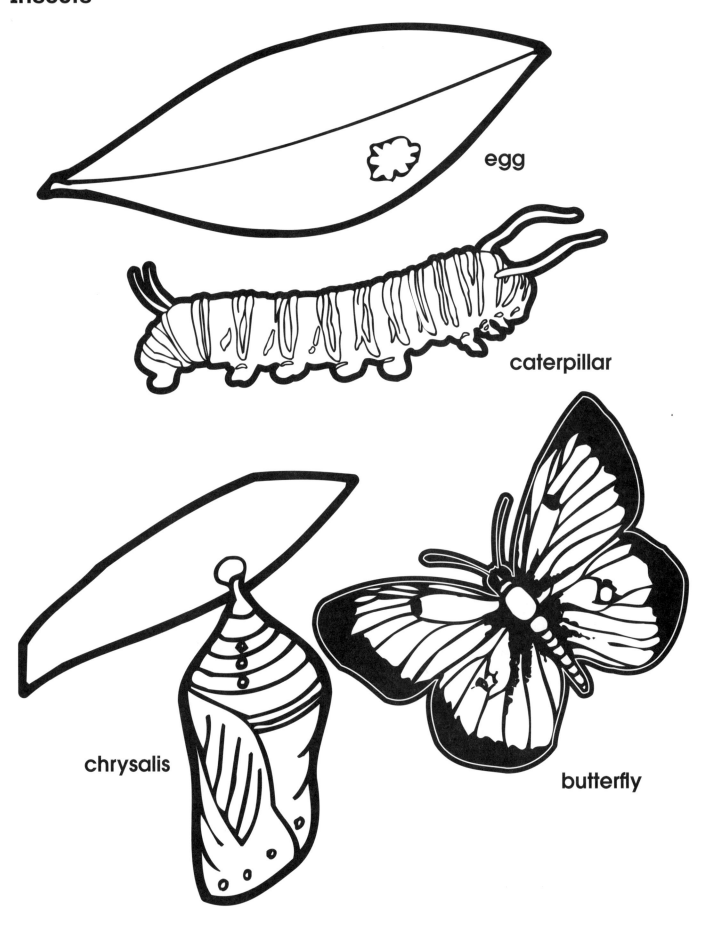

egg

caterpillar

chrysalis

butterfly

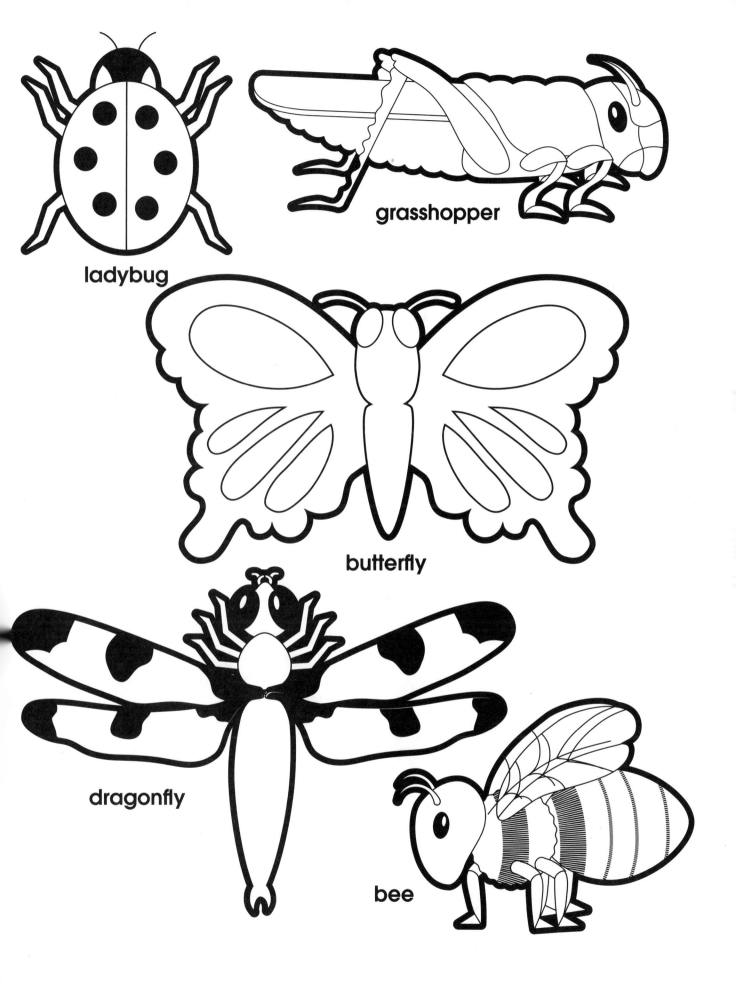

ladybug

grasshopper

butterfly

dragonfly

bee

Kwanzaa

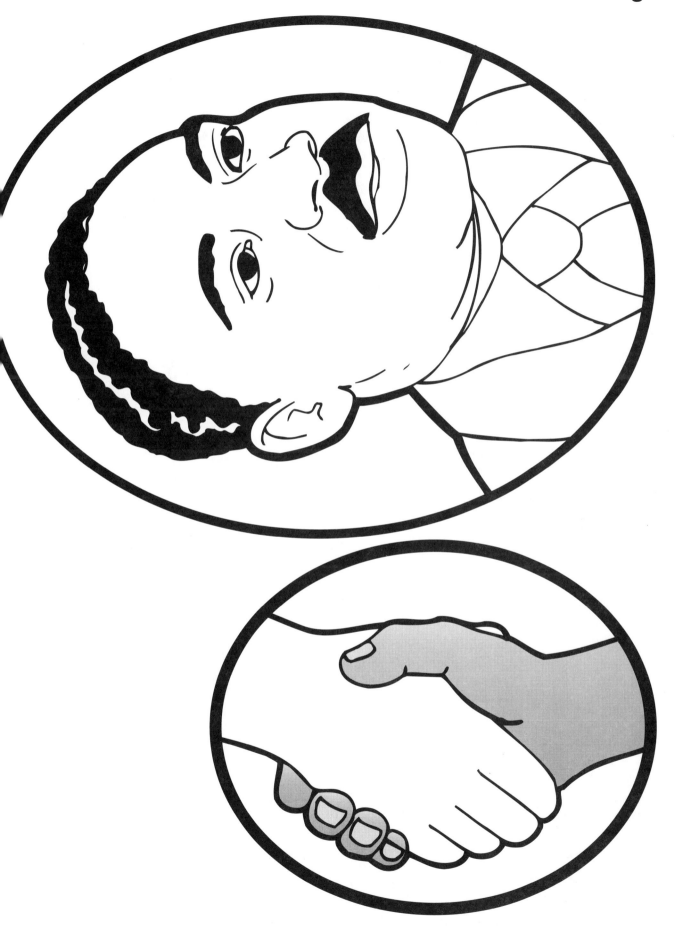

Money

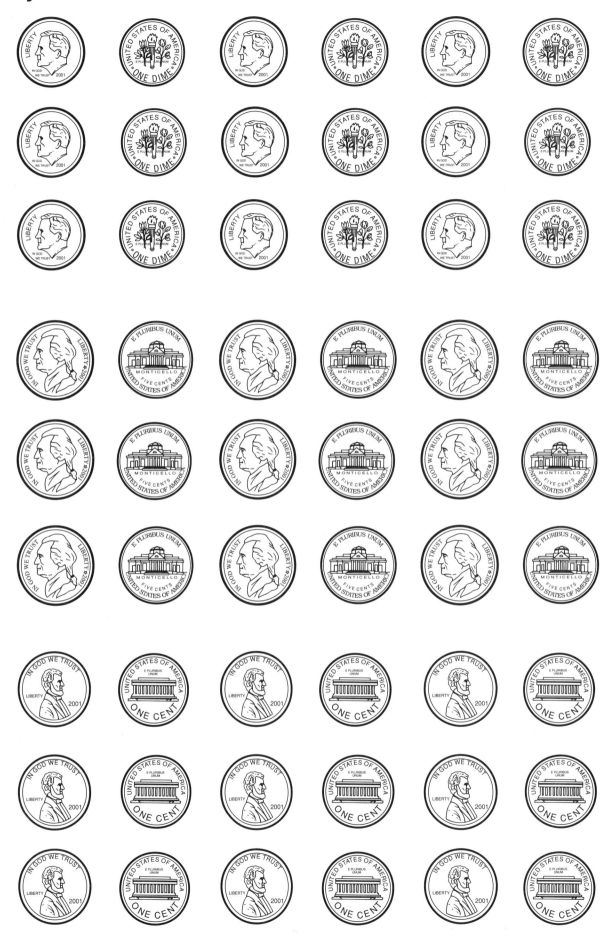

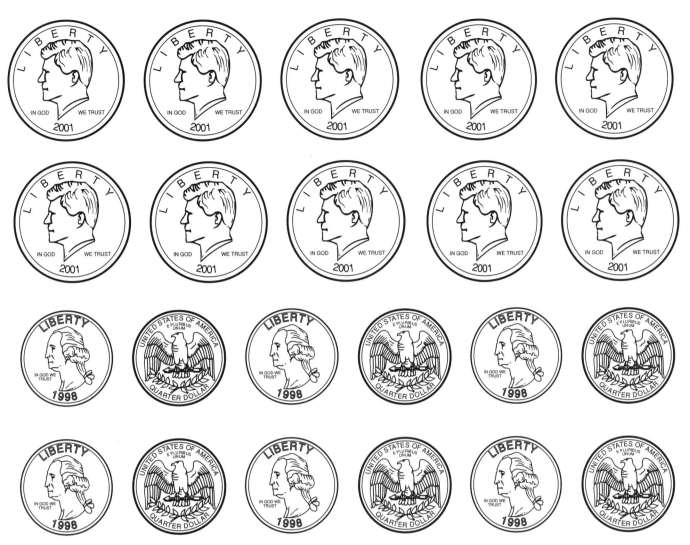

98 ©The Education Center, Inc. • *Big Book of Patterns* • TEC61225

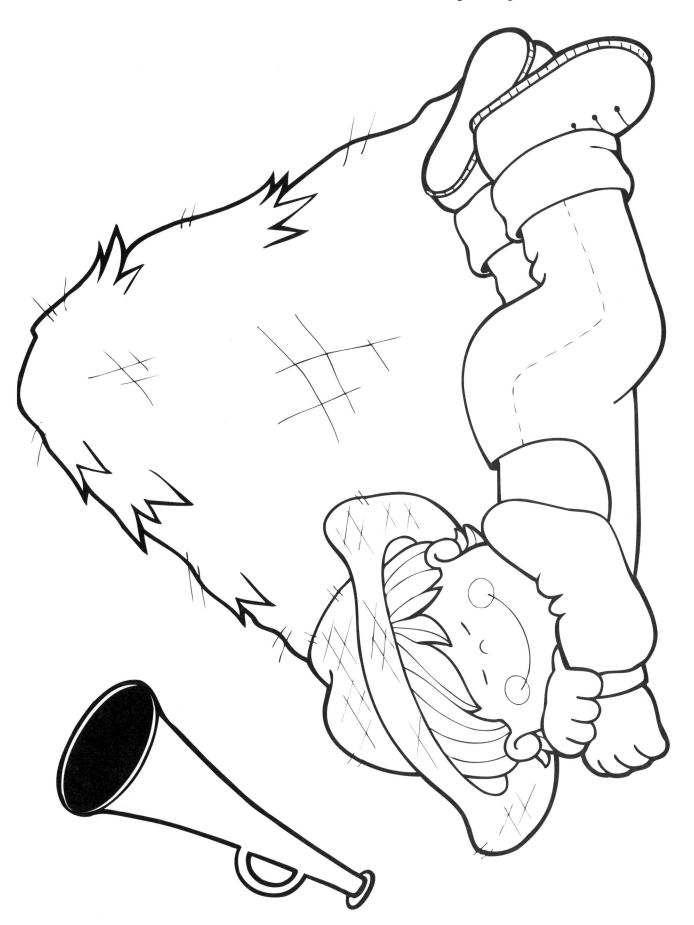

©The Education Center, Inc. • *Big Book of Patterns* • TEC61225

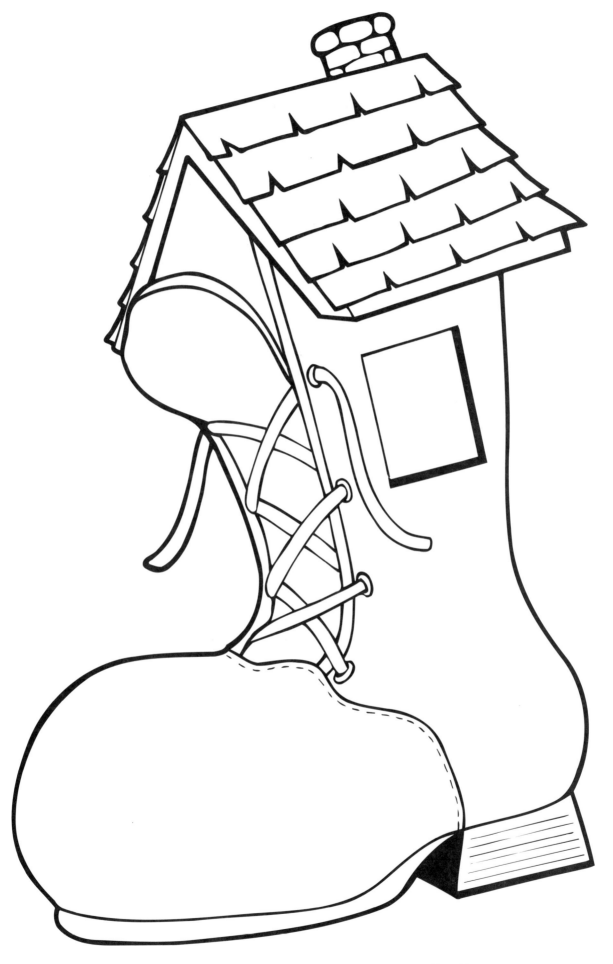

107

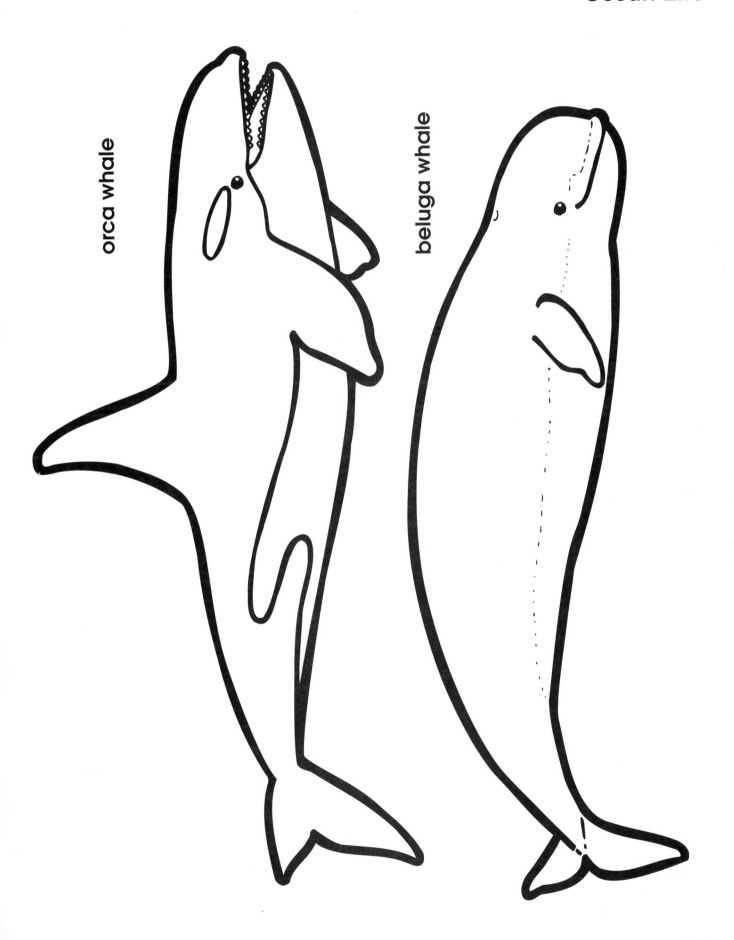

orca whale

beluga whale

bottle-nosed dolphin

white shark

118 ©The Education Center, Inc. • *Big Book of Patterns* • TEC61225

122   ©The Education Center, Inc. • *Big Book of Patterns* • TEC61225

124

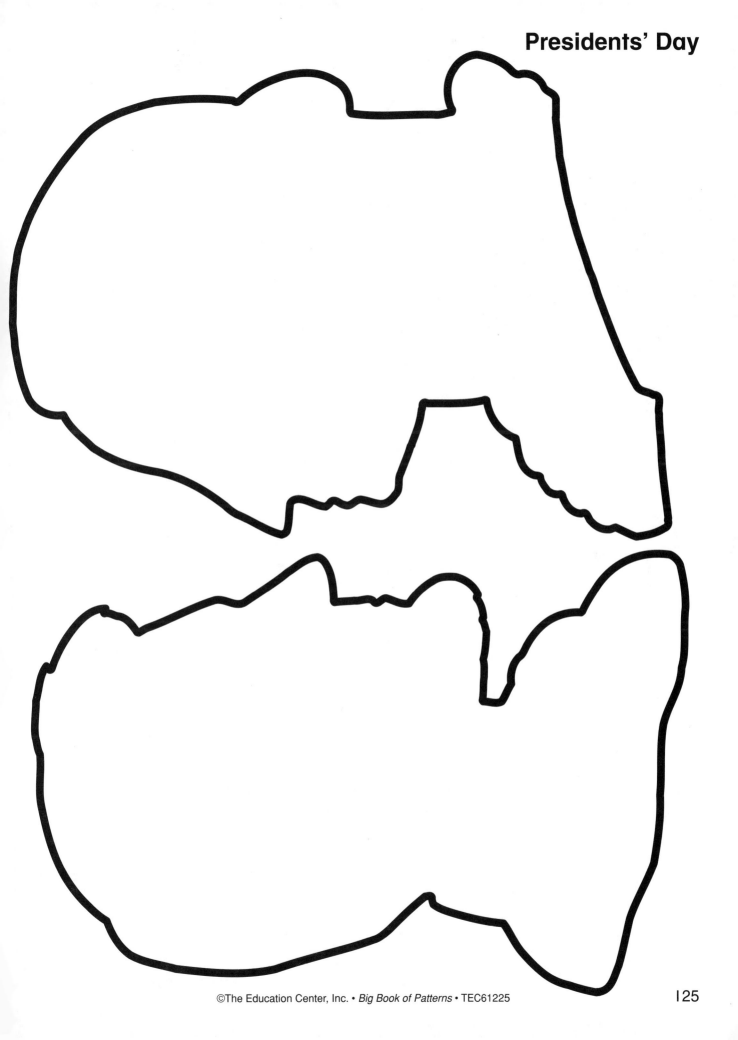

Shapes

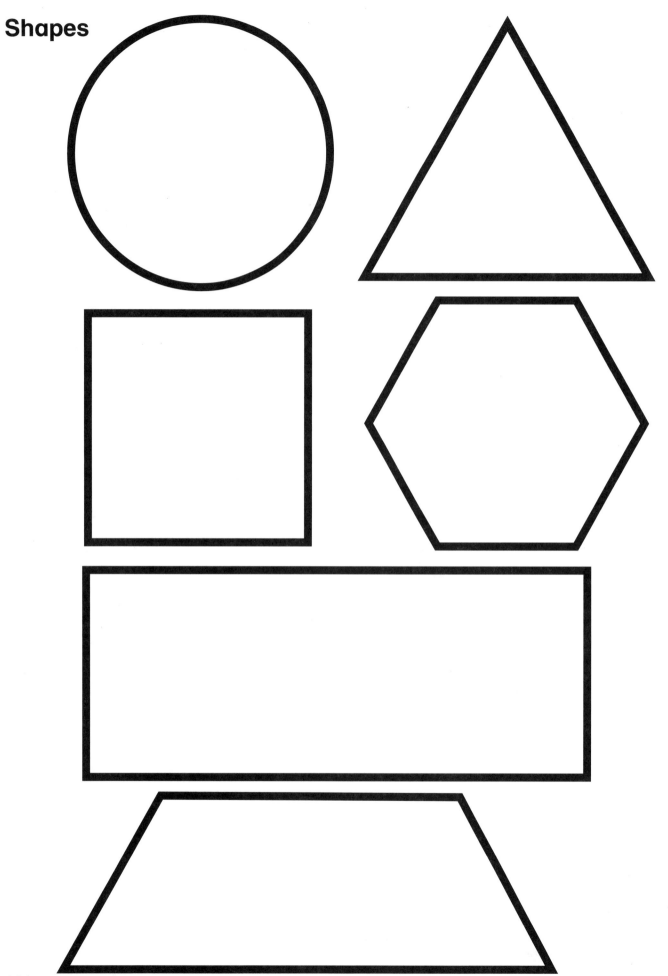

128

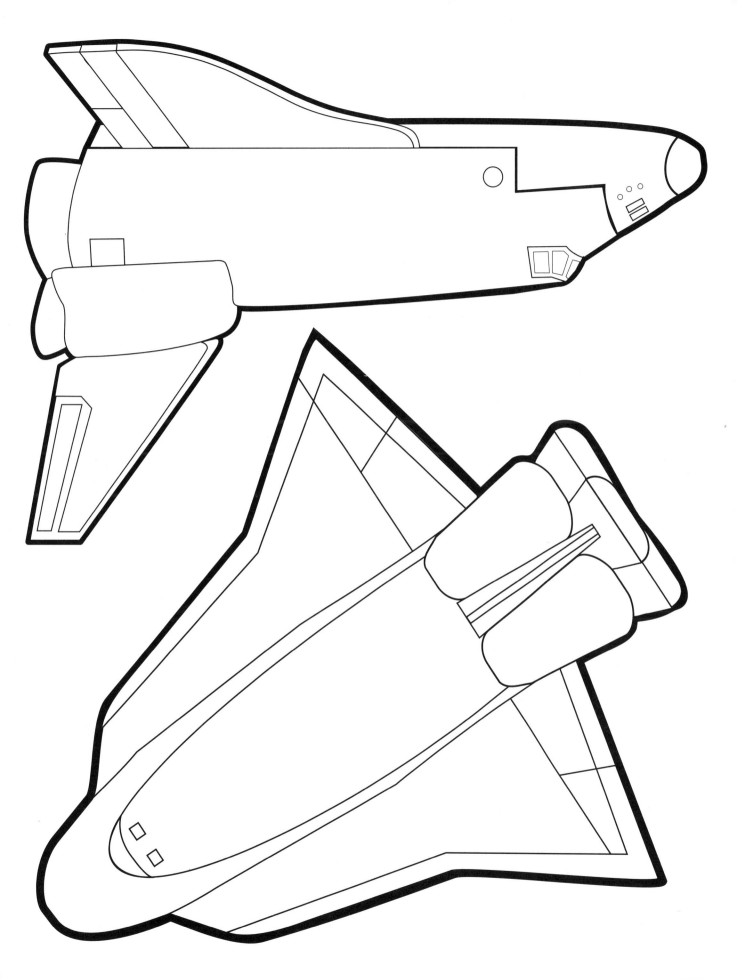

Spiders

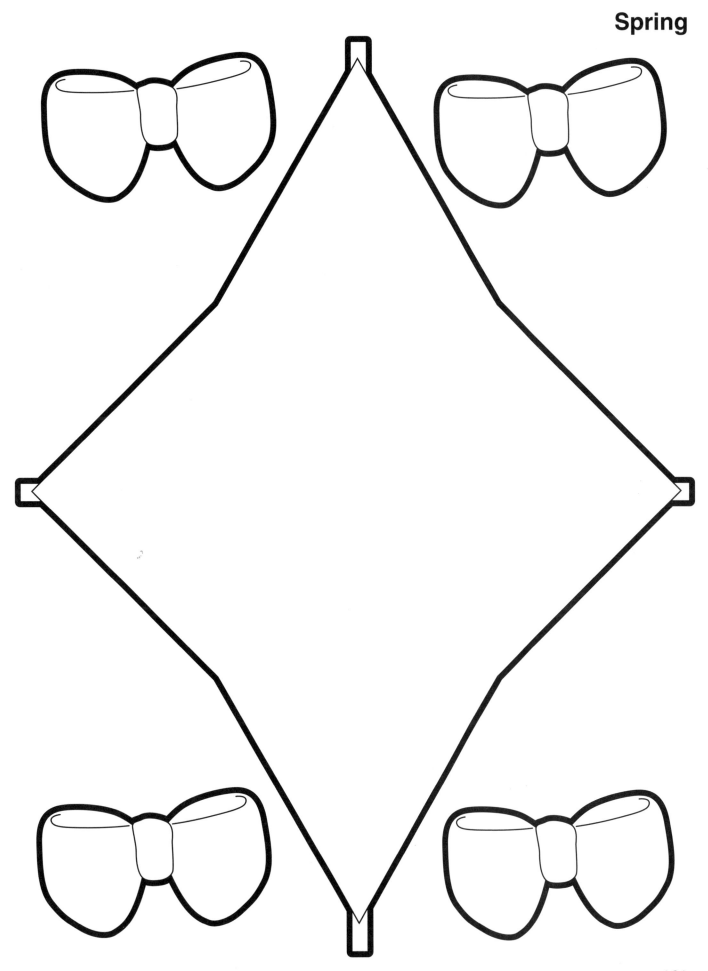

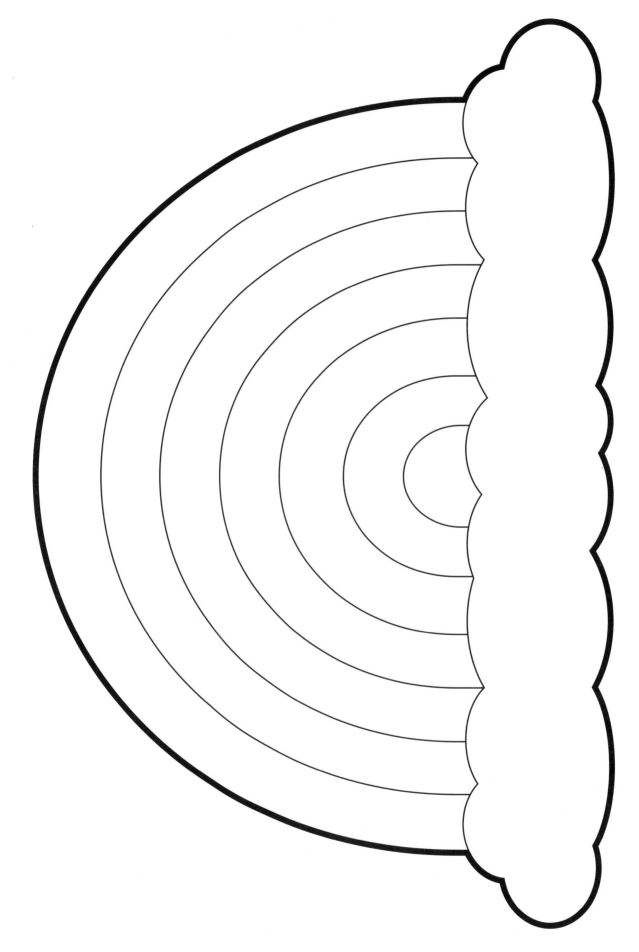

132

133

136

138

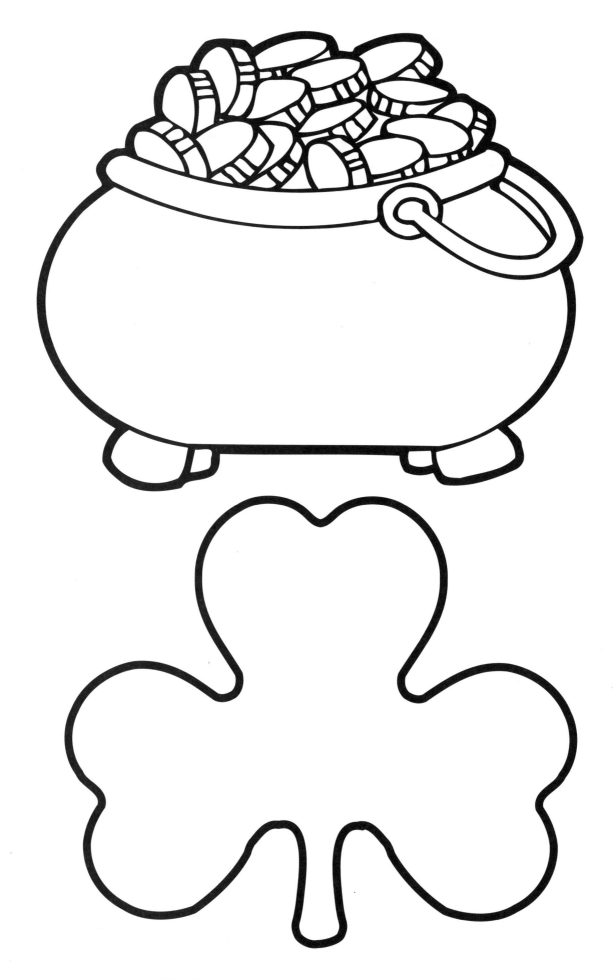

148

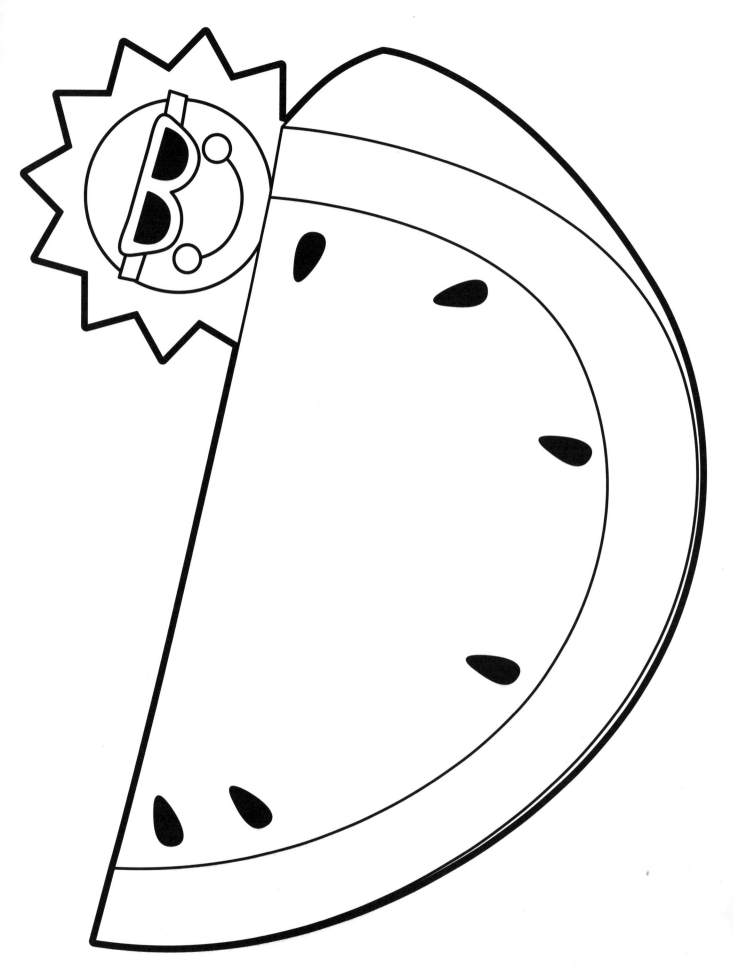

150

152

154 ©The Education Center, Inc. • *Big Book of Patterns* • TEC61225

156

Teddy Bears

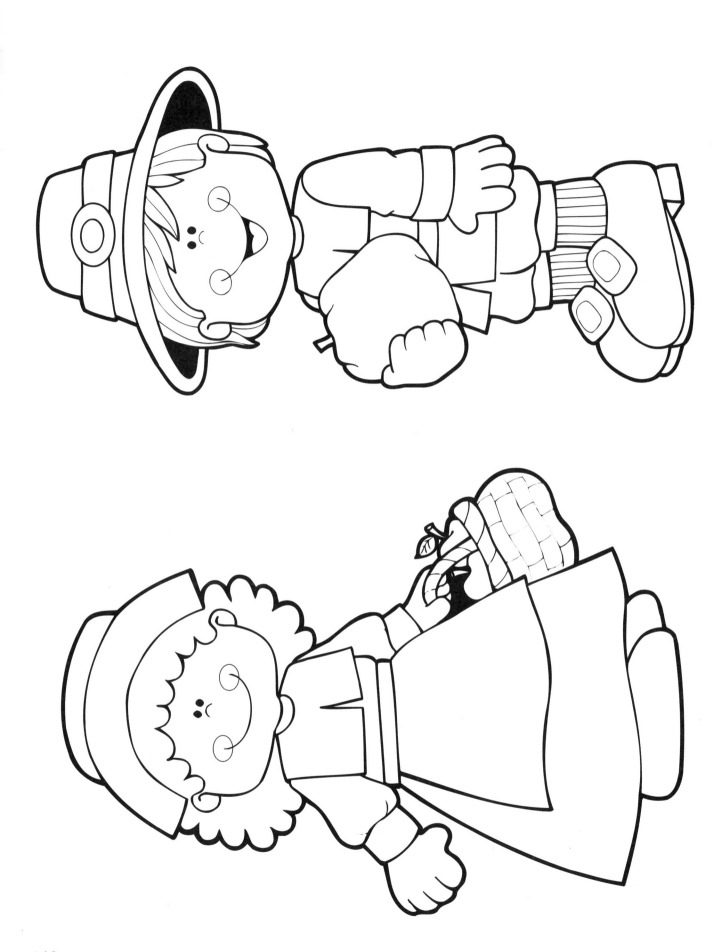

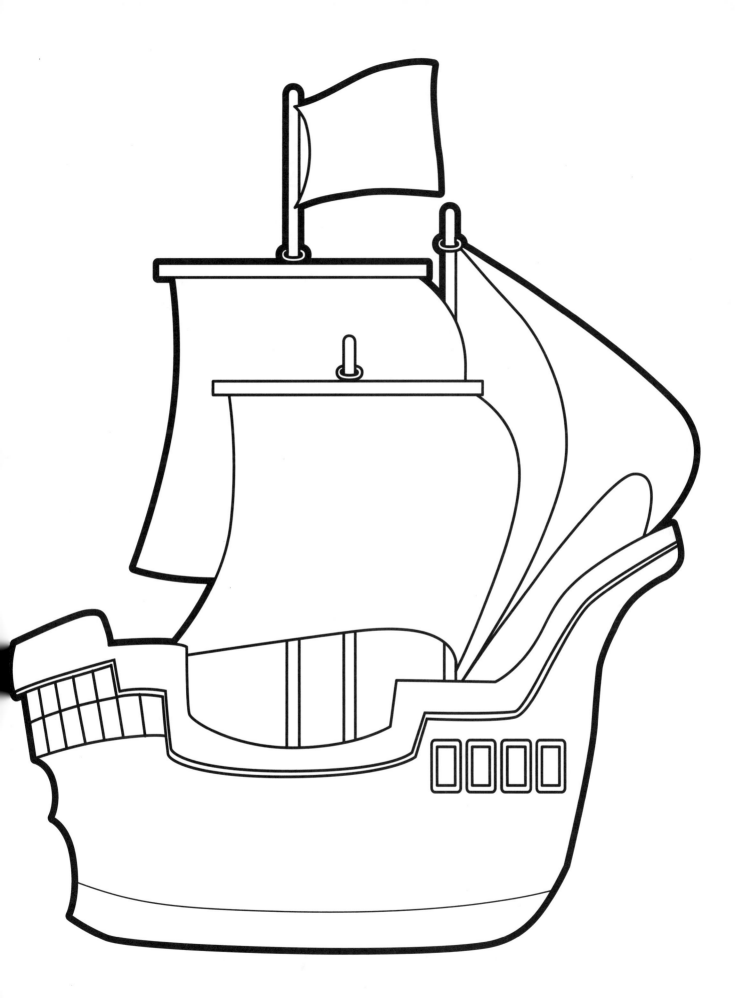

Time

minute hand · hour hand

Transportation

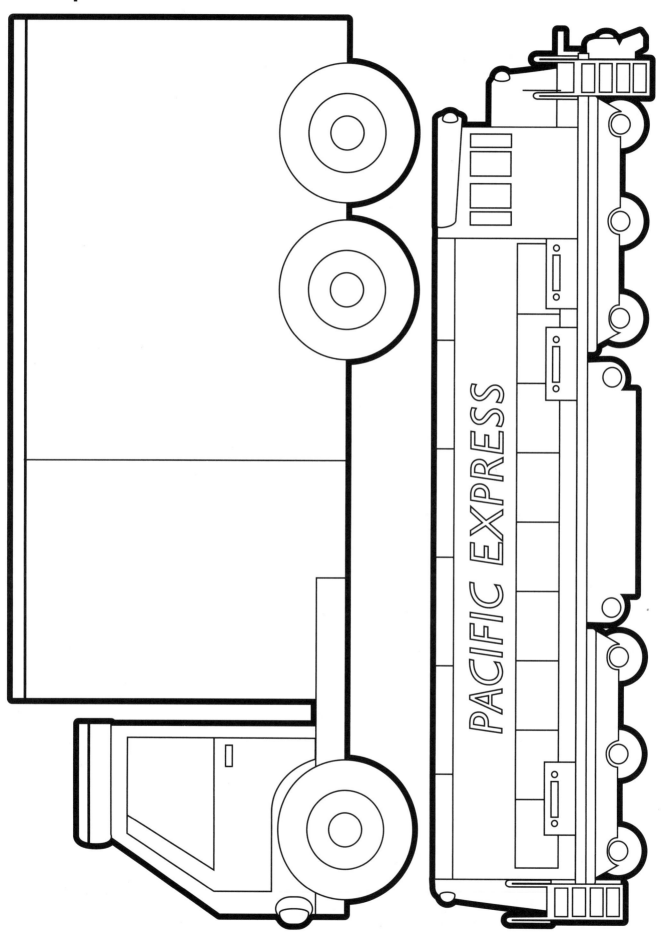

PACIFIC EXPRESS

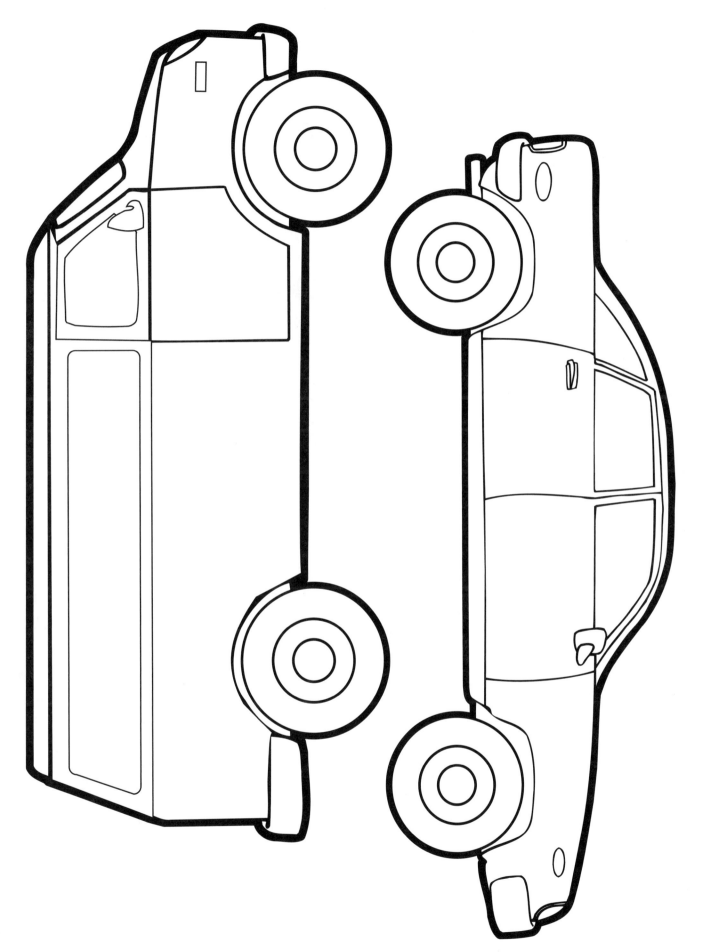

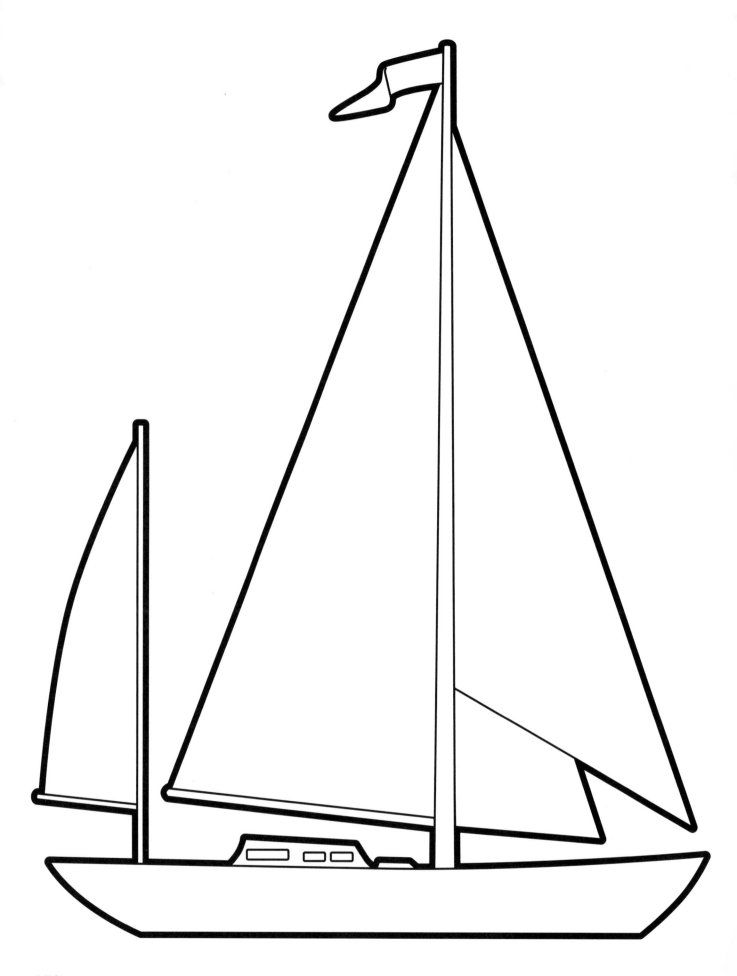

174 ©The Education Center, Inc. • *Big Book of Patterns* • TEC61225

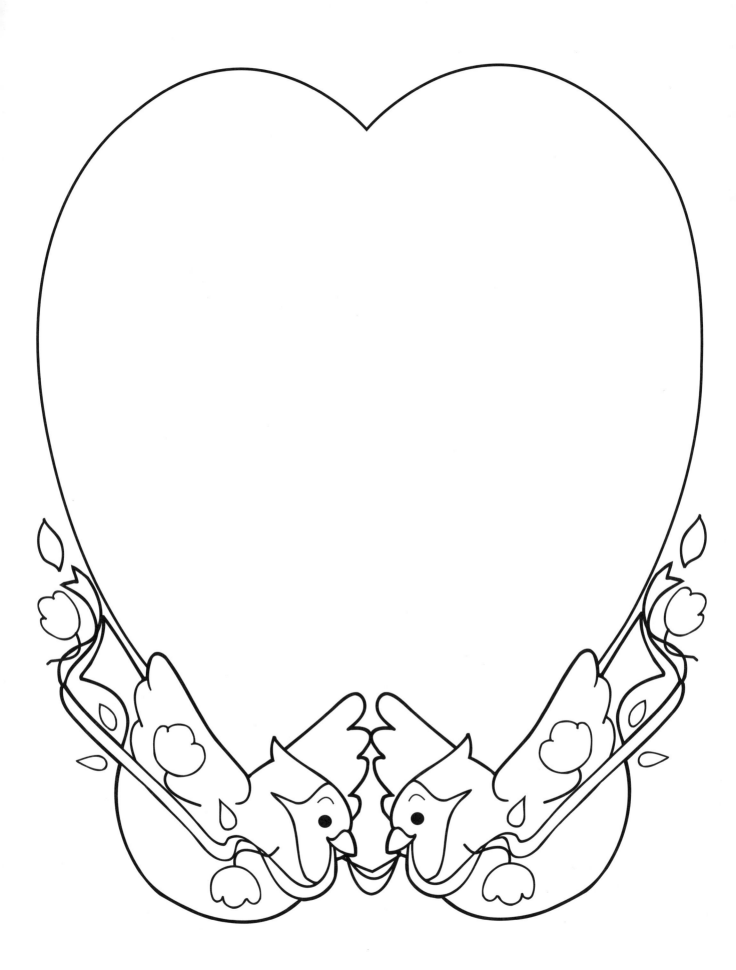

CUTIE

LOVE

BE MINE

Weather

sunny

partly cloudy

cloudy

rain

lightning

snow

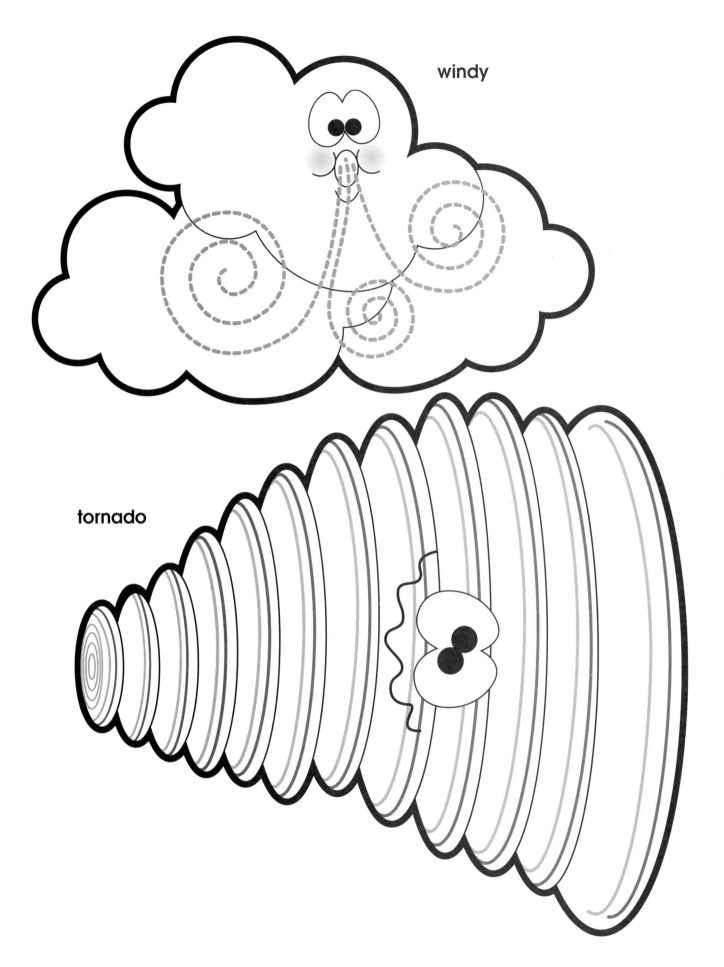

windy

tornado

186

Wild West

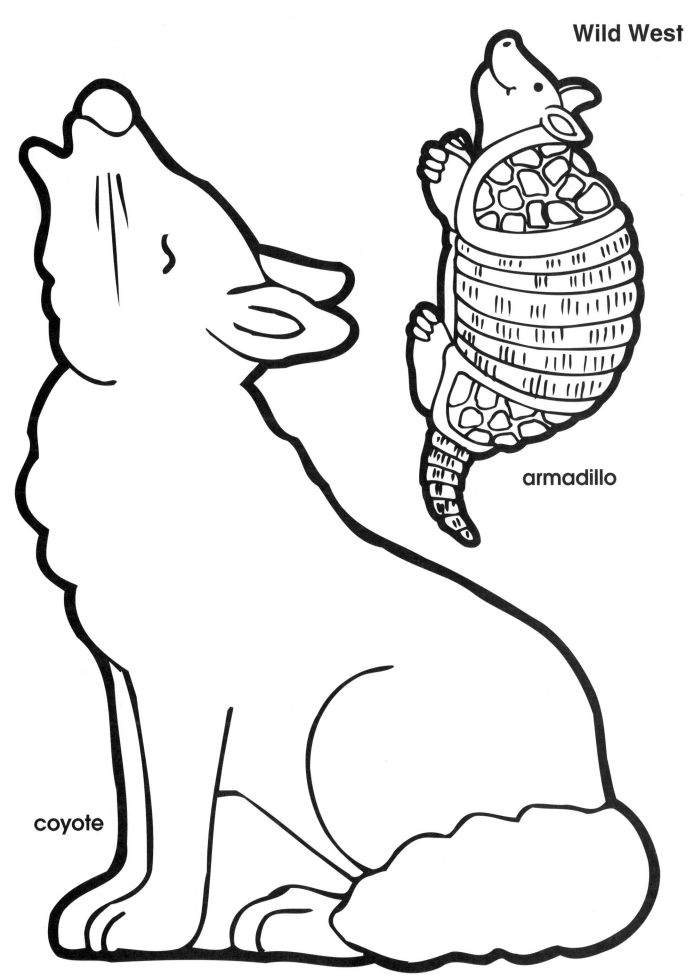

armadillo

coyote

©The Education Center, Inc. • *Big Book of Patterns* • TEC61225

187

buffalo

rattlesnake

jackrabbit

prairie dog

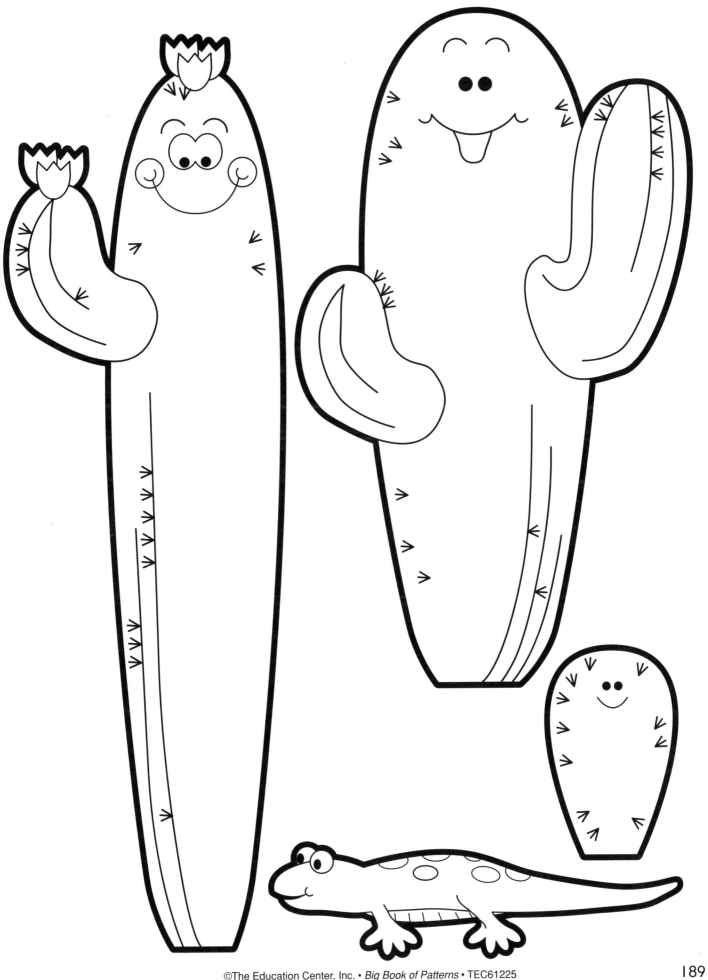

192 ©The Education Center, Inc. • *Big Book of Patterns* • TEC61225

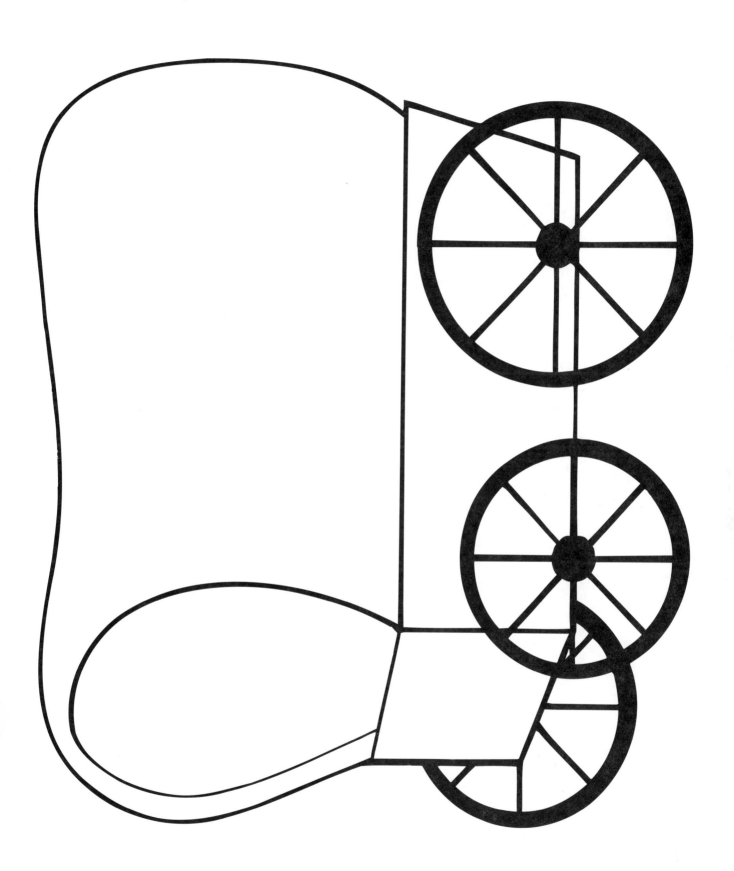

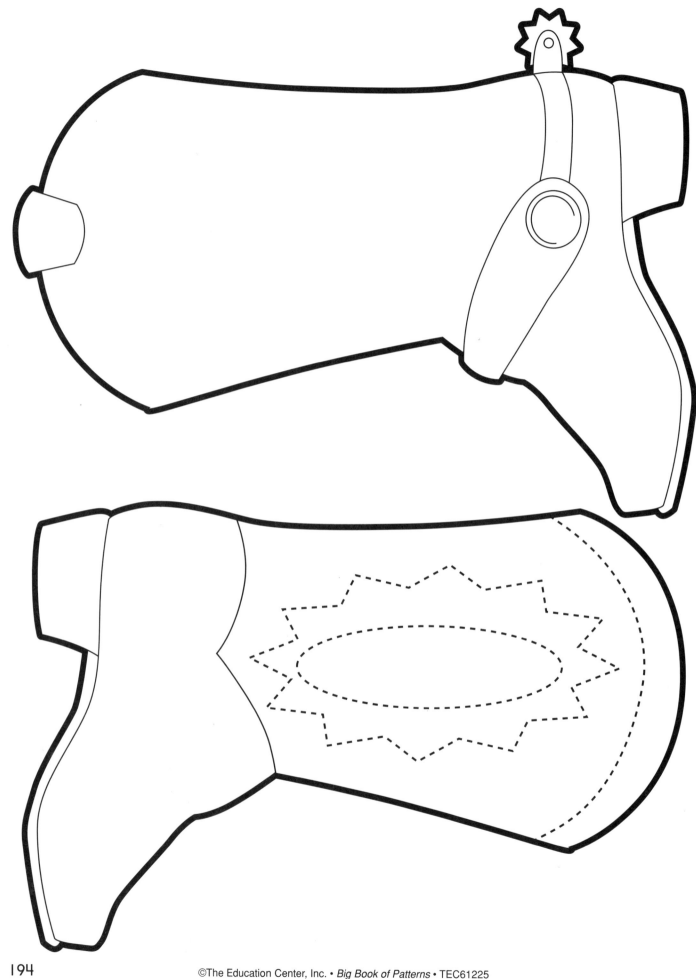

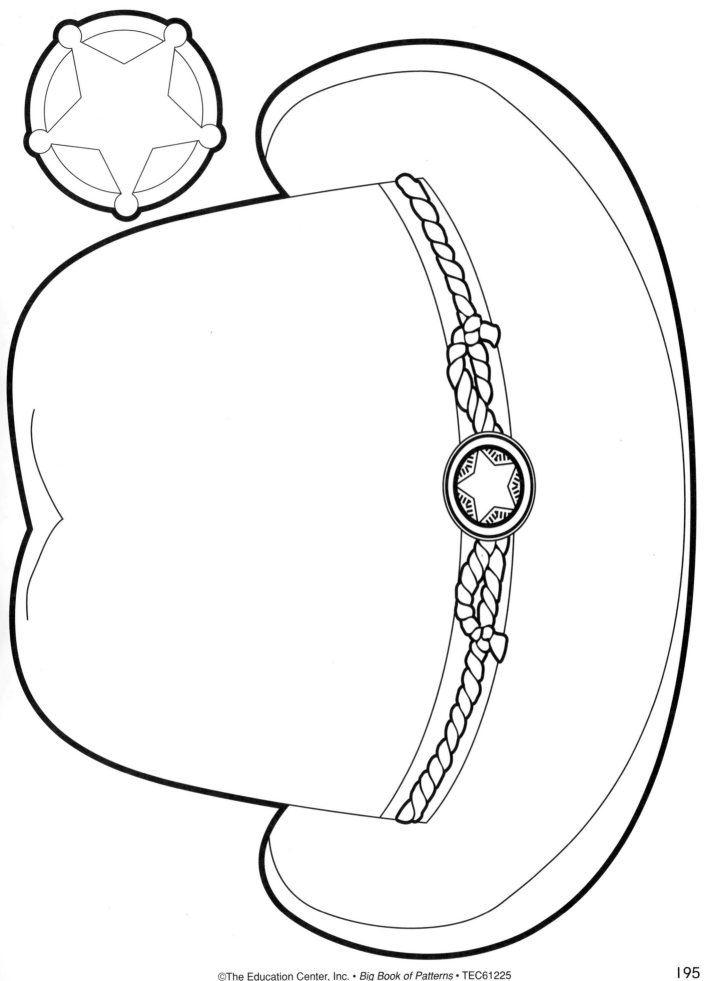

200   ©The Education Center, Inc. • *Big Book of Patterns* • TEC61225

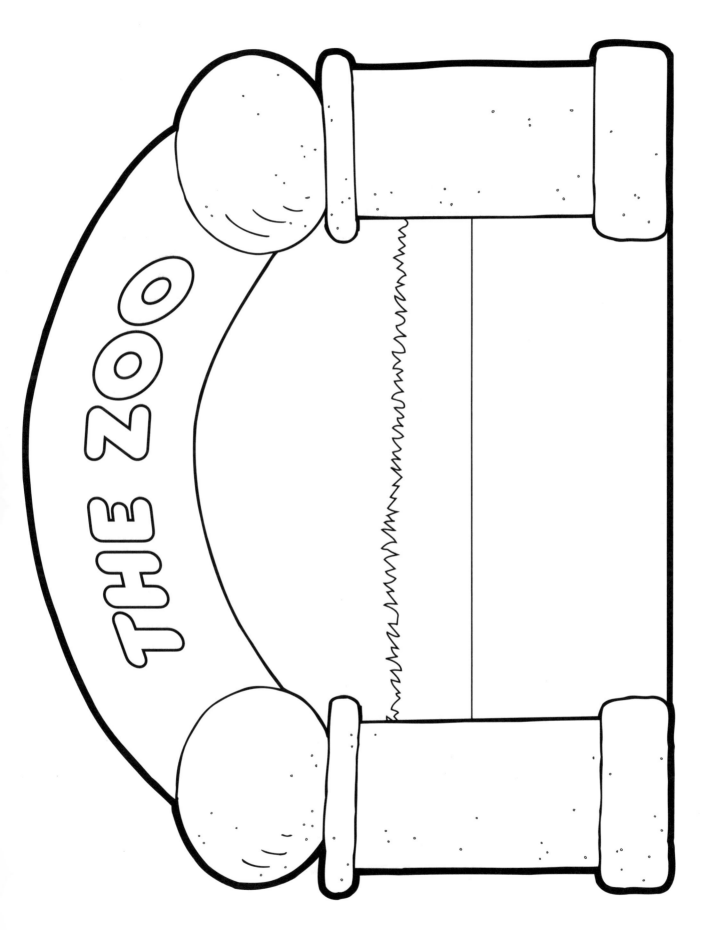

THE ZOO

204

208